LOOG GUITAR FOR KIDS

Christmas Carols, Classical Music, Nursery Rhymes, Traditional & Folk Songs!

LOOG GUITAR FOR KIDS:

Christmas Carols, Classical Music, Nursery Rhymes, Traditional & Folk Songs!

© JAVIER MARCÓ

ISBN-13:978-1718894099
ISBN-10:1718894090

CONTENTS

Playing guide

Notation
In this book, two methods of music notation are presented: standard notation and tablature.

Tablature
Tablature indicates the position of the notes on the fretboard. There are three lines, one for each string.

The number placed on a line indicates the fret location of a note.

This indicates the 3rd fret of the first string: a G note.

This indicates the 1st fret of the second string: a C note.

This indicates the third string open: a G note.

Standard notation
Notes are written on a Staff.

Staff
The staff consists of five lines and four spaces, on which notes symbols are placed.

Clef
A clef assigns an individual note to a certain line.

The **Treble Clef** or **G Clef** is used for the Loog Guitar.

This clef indicates the position of the note G which is on the second line from the bottom.

Note

A note is a sign used to represent the relative pitch of a sound.
There are seven notes: A, B, C, D, E, F and G.

Notes on Treble Clef:

Ledger lines

The ledger lines are used to inscribe notes outside the lines and spaces of the staff.

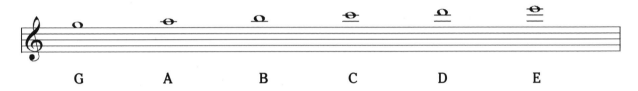

Accidentals

An accidental is a symbol to raise or lower the pitch of a note.

♯ sharp   Next note up half step.

♭ flat   Next note down half step.

♮ natural   Cancels a flat or a sharp.

Note values

A **note value** is used to indicate the duration of a note. A **rest** is an interval of silence, marked by a sign indicating the length of the pause. Each rest corresponds to a particular note value.

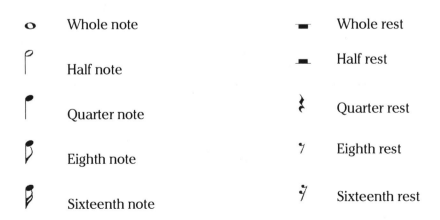

Dotted note

A dotted note is a note with a small dot written after it. The dot adds half as much again to the basic note's duration.

Tie

A tie is a curved line connecting the heads of two notes of the same pitch, indicating that they are to be played as a single note with a duration equal to the sum of the individual notes' note values.

Bars or Measures

The staff is divided into equal segments of time consisting of the same number of beats, called bar or measures.

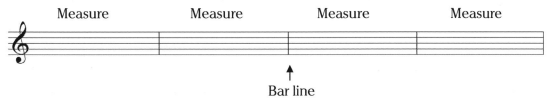

Time signature

Time signature consists of two numbers, the upper number specifies how many beats (or counts) are in each measure, and the lower number tells us the note value which represents one beat.

Example: 4/4 means four quarters, or four beats per measure with a quarter note receiving one beat or count.

Key signature

A Key signature is a group of accidentals, generally written at the beginning of a score immediately after the clef, and shows which notes always get sharps or flats. Accidentals on the lines and spaces in the key signature affect those notes throughout the piece unless there is a natural sign.

Repeat sign

The repeat sign indicates a section should be repeated from the beginning, and then continue on. A corresponding sign facing the other way indicates where the repeat is to begin.

First and second endings
The section should be repeated from the beginning, and number brackets above the bars indicate which to played the first time (1), which to play the second time (2).

Dynamics
Dynamics refers to the volume of the notes.

p (piano), meaning soft.
mp (mezzo-piano), meaning "moderately soft".
mf (mezzo-forte), meaning "moderately loud".
f (forte), meaning loud.

Crescendo. A gradual increase in volume.

Decrescendo. A gradual decrease in volume.

Tempo Markings
Tempo is written at the beginning of a piece of music and indicates how slow or fast this piece should be played.

Lento — very slow (40–60 bpm)
Adagio — slow and stately (66–76 bpm)
Andate — at a walking pace (76–108 bpm)
Moderato — moderately (101-110 bpm)
Allegretto — moderately fast (but less so than allegro)
Allegro — fast, quickly and bright (120–139 bpm)
Presto — extremely fast (180–200 bpm)

Alla marcia — in the manner of a march
In tempo di valse — in tempo of vals

rallentando — gradual slowing down
a tempo — returns to the base tempo after a *rallentando*

Articulation

Legato. Notes are played smoothly and connected.

Stacatto. Notes are played separated or detached from its neighbours by a silence.

Fermata (pause)

The note is to be prolonged at the pleasure of the performer.

Fingering

In this book **left hand fingering** is indicated using numbers above the staff.

0= open
1= index
2= middle
3= ring
4= little finger

-Roman numbers indicates fret position for bars

CI = full bar, first fret.
cII = half bar, second fret.

Solid lines indicates how long to hold the bar.

Aloutte

Traditionnel

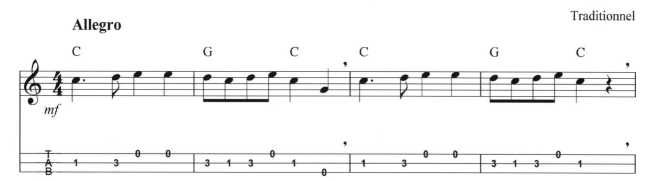

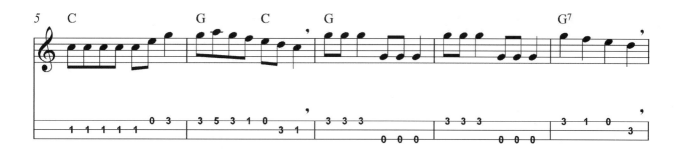

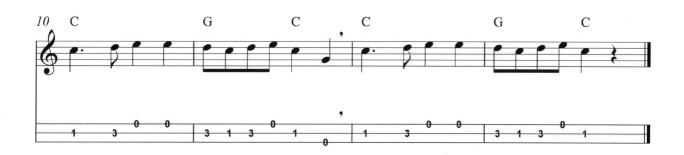

Amazing Grace

Traditional

Andante

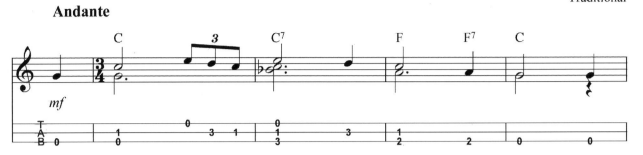

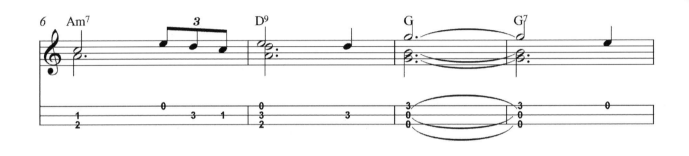

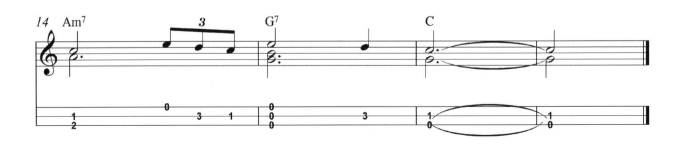

America The Beautiful

Music by Samuel A. Ward

Moderato

Arroz Con Leche

Tradicional

Aserrín, Aserrán

Tradicional

Allegro

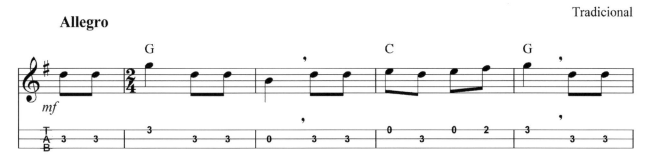

Aura Lee

George R. Poulton

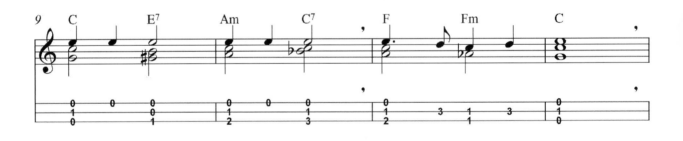

16

Cielito Lindo

Quirino Mendoza y Cortés

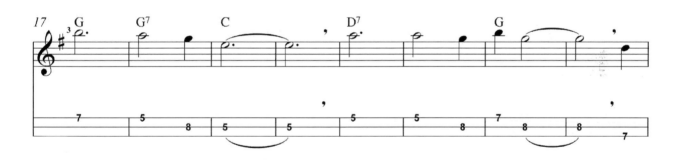

For He's a Jolly Good Fellow

Traditional

Allegro

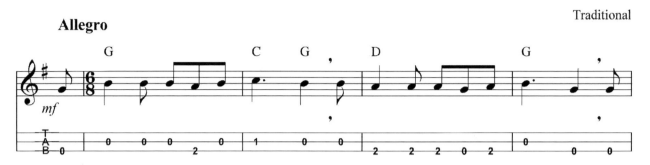

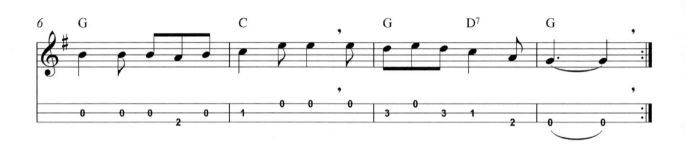

Frere Jacques

Traditionnel

Allegro

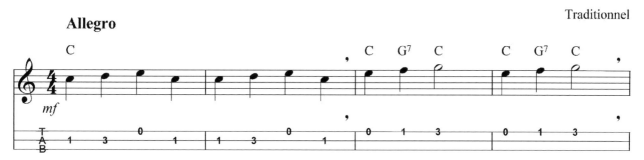

Go Tell Aunt Rhody

Traditional

Allegro

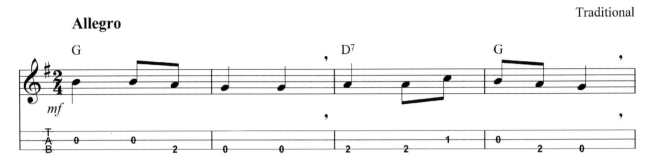

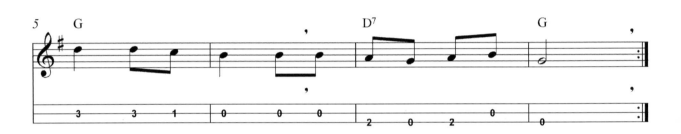

Good Morning To All

Patty & Mildred J. Hill

Allegro

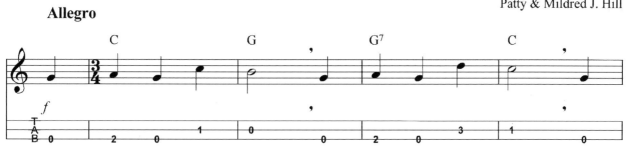

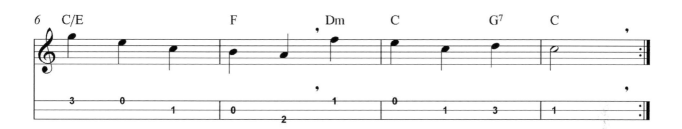

Greensleeves

Traditional English Folk Song

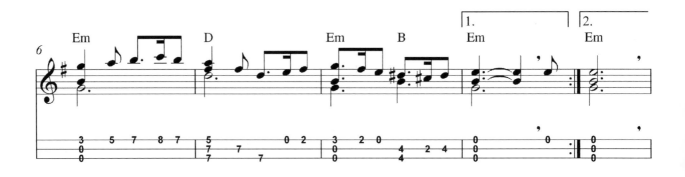

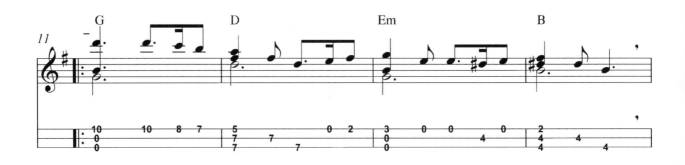

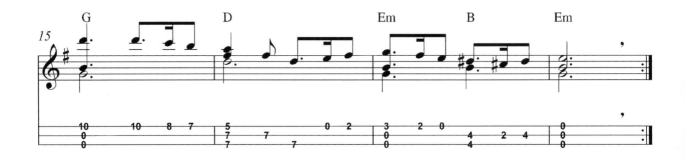

Jingle Bells

James Lord Pierpont

La Cucaracha

Tradicional

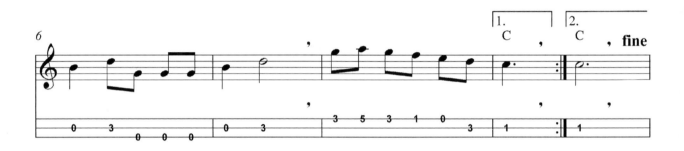

La Donna è Mobile

Giuseppe Verdi

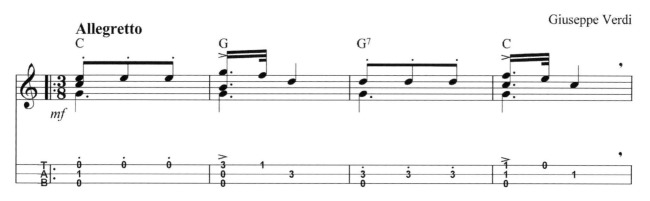

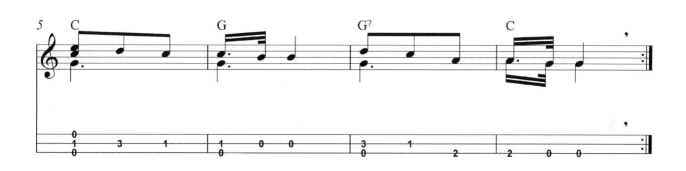

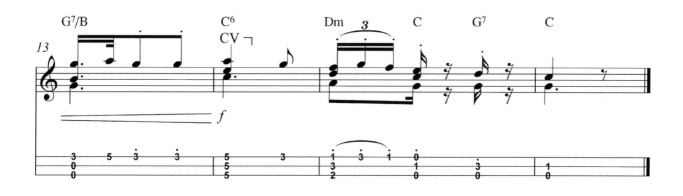

Las Mañanitas

Tradicional

Allegro

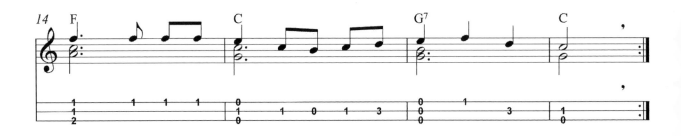

London Bridge Is Falling Down

Traditional

Allegro

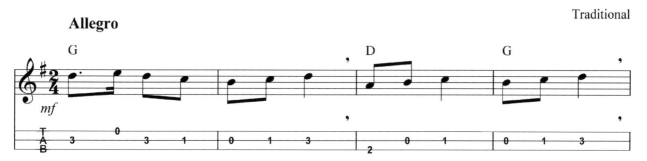

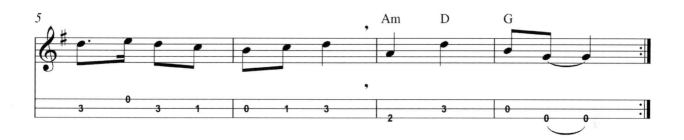

Mary Had A Little Lamb

Traditional

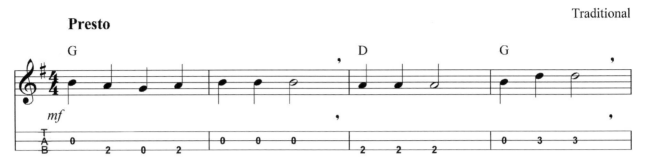

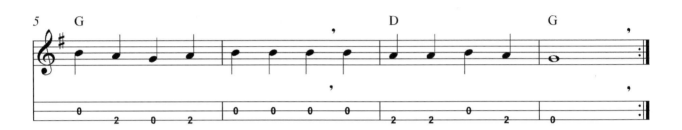

Menuett, BWV Anh 114

Johann Sebastian Bach

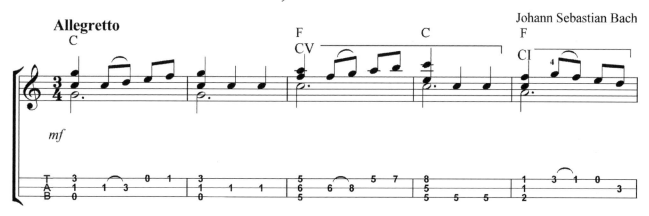

My Bonnie Lies Over The Ocean

Traditional

Allegro

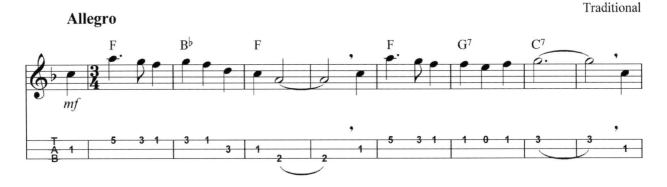

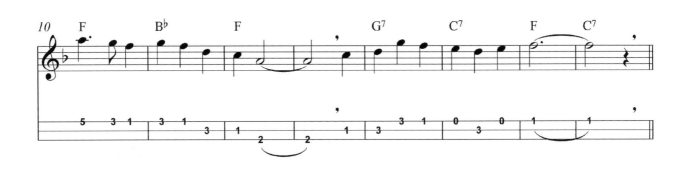

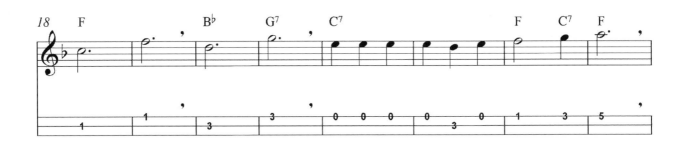

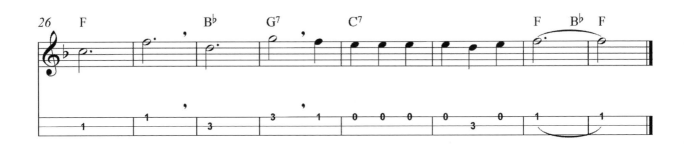

Ode an die Freude, Op. 125

Ludwig Van Beethoven

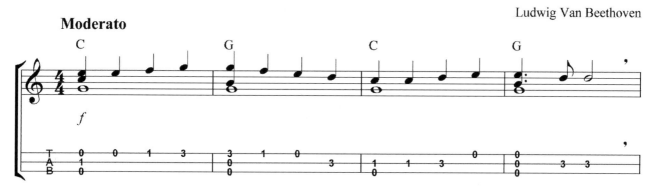

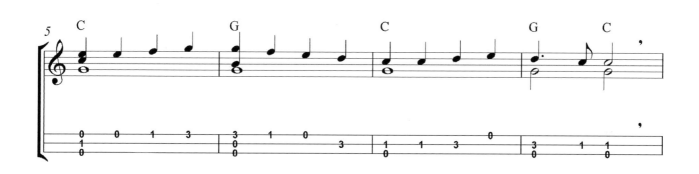

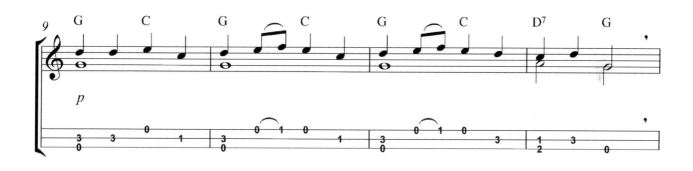

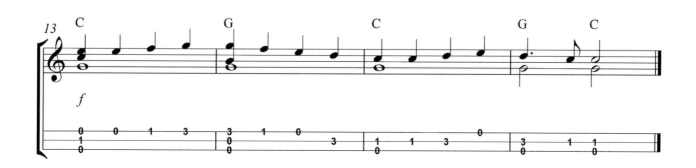

Oh! Susanna

Stephen Foster

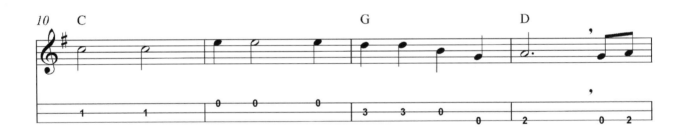

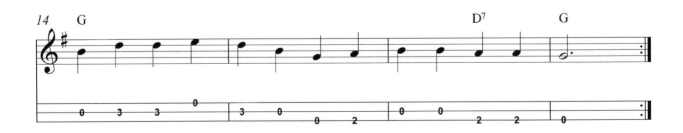

Old MacDonald Had a Farm

Traditional

Presto

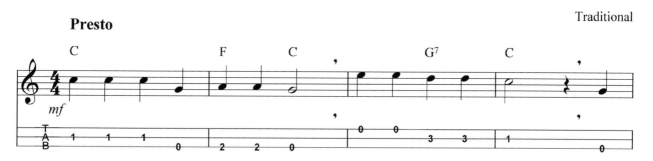

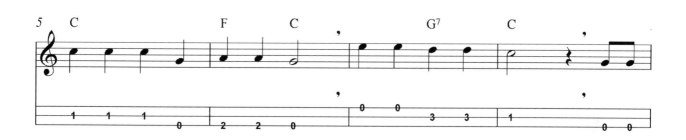

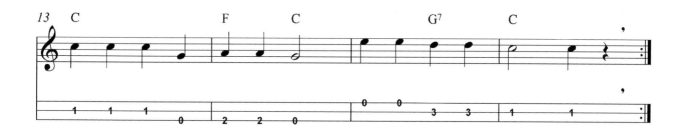

Row Row Row Your Boat

Traditional

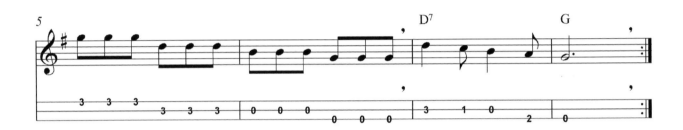

Scarborough Fair

Traditional

Allegro

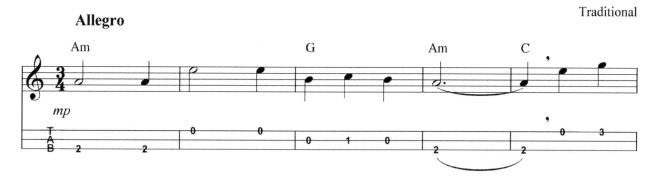

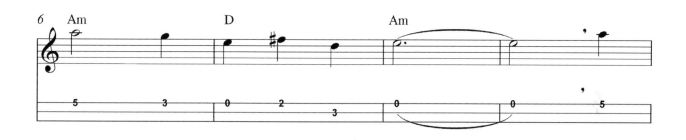

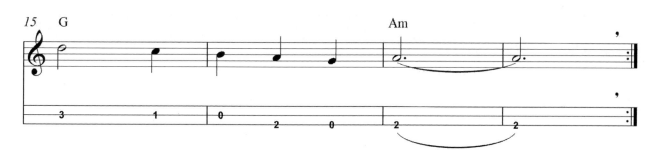

Stille Nacht, heilige Nacht

Franz Xaver Gruber

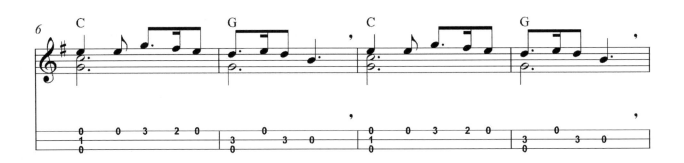

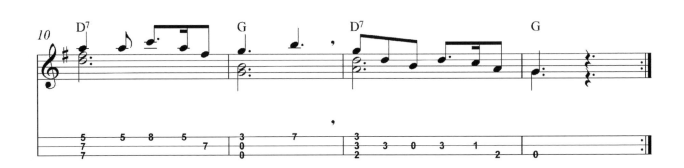

Sur le Pont d'Avignon

Traditionnel

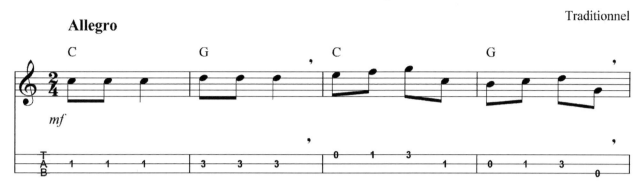

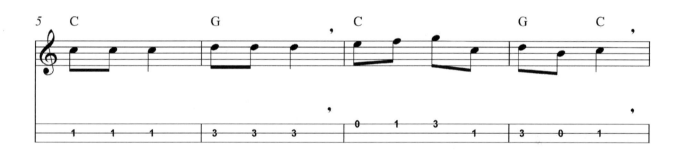

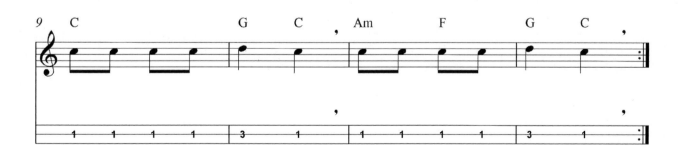

The House Of The Rising Sun

Traditional

Moderato

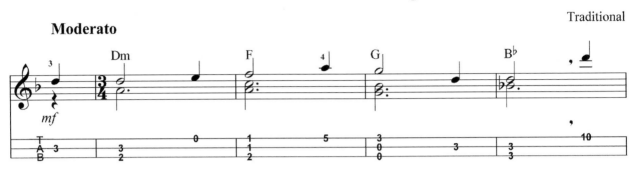

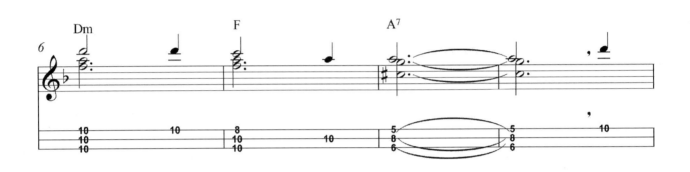

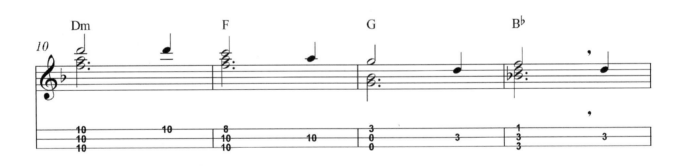

The Star-Spangled Banner

Music by John Stafford Smith

Moderato

Twinkle Twinkle Little Star

W. A. Mozart

Moderato

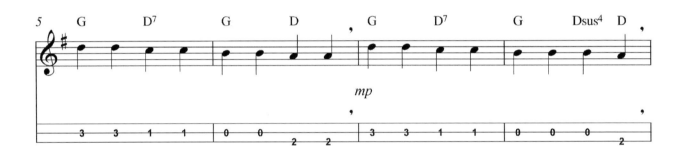

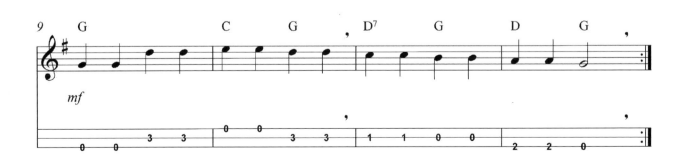

Un Elefante Se Balanceaba

Tradicional

Allegro

We Wish You A Merry Christmas

Traditional

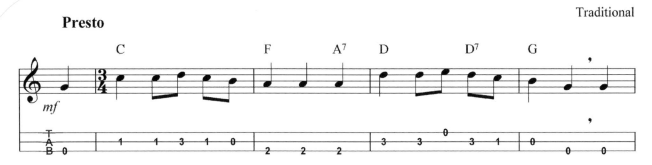

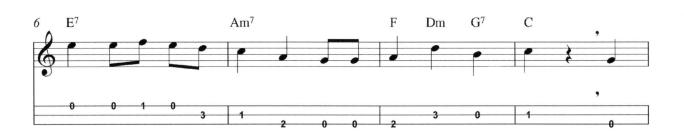

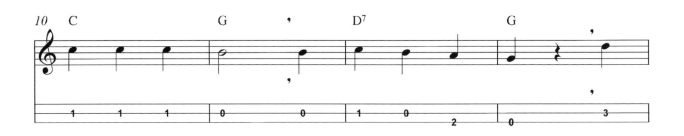

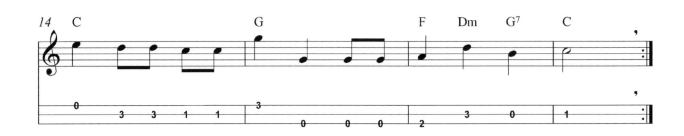

When Johnny Comes Marching Home

Traditional

Allegro

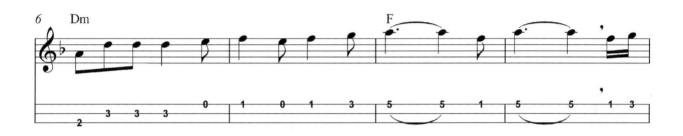

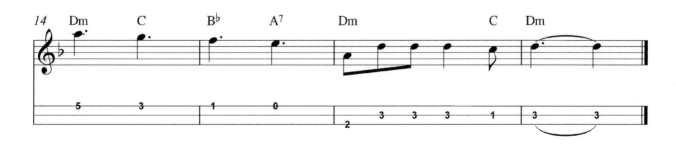

When The Saints Go Marching In

Traditional

Presto

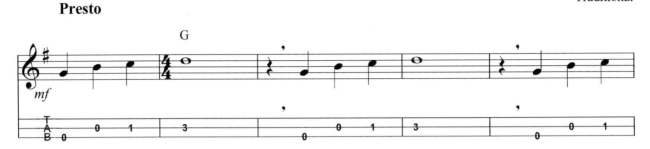

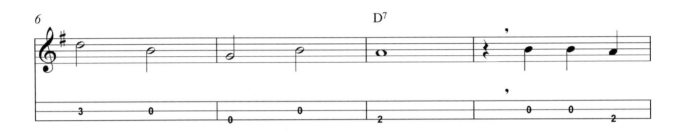

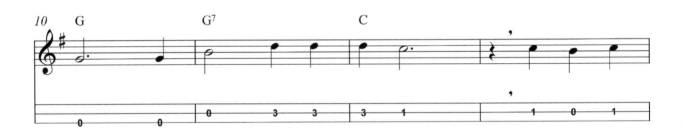

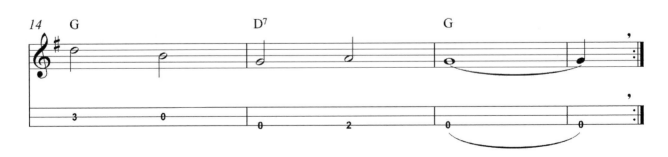

Guten Abend, gut' Nacht

Johannes Brahms

Adagio

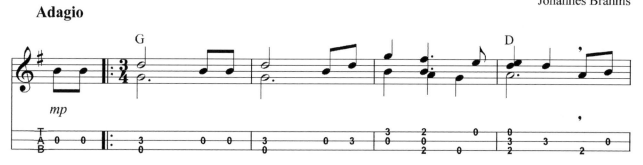

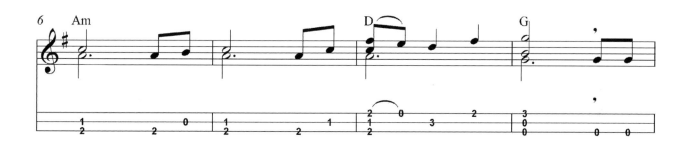

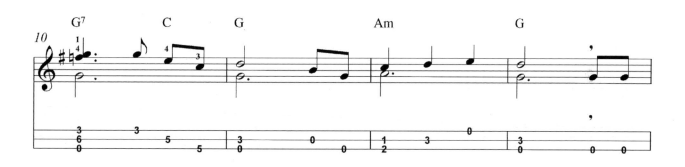

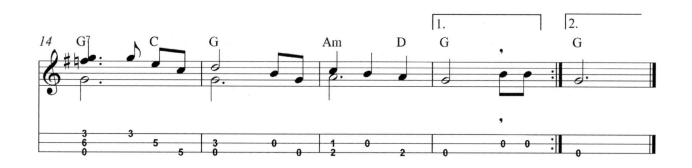

Yankee Doodle

Traditional

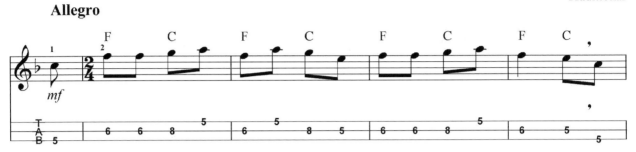

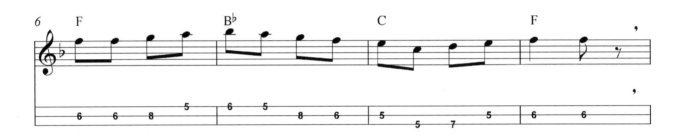

info@marcomusica.com

Made in the USA
Columbia, SC
17 November 2021

• LOOG GUITAR FOR KIDS •

Aloutte
Amazing Grace
America The Beautiful
Arroz Con Leche
Aserrin, Aserran
Aura Lee
Cielito Lindo
For He's a Jolly Good Fellow
Frere Jacques
Go Tell Aunt Rhody
Good Morning To All
Greensleeves
Jingle Bells
La Cucaracha
La Donna e Mobile
Las Mañanitas
London Bridge Is Falling Down
Mary Had A Little Lamb
Menuett in G
My Bonnie Lies Over The Ocean
Ode an die Freude
Oh! Susanna
Old MacDonald Had a Farm
Row Row Row Your Boat
Scarborough Fair
Stille Nacht, heilige Nacht
Sur le Pont d'Avignon
The House Of The Rising Sun
The Star-Spangled Banner
Twinkle Twinkle Little Star
Un Elefante Se Balanceaba
We Wish You A Merry Christmas
When Johnny Comes Marching Home
When the Saints Go Marching In
Wiegenlied
Yankee Doodle

ISBN 9781718894099

9 781718 894099

McDonnell Douglas
MD-11

A Long Beach Swansong

Arthur A C Steffen